HEAVEN STUDY GUIDE

HEAVEN
STUDY GUIDE

RANDY
ALCORN

TYNDALE HOUSE PUBLISHERS, INC.
CAROL STREAM, ILLINOIS

Visit Tyndale's exciting Web site at www.tyndale.com.

TYNDALE and Tyndale's quill logo are registered trademarks of Tyndale House Publishers, Inc.

Heaven Study Guide

Designed by Jessie McGrath

ISBN 978-1-4143-0977-4

Printed in the United States of America

16 15 14 13 12 11 10
11 10 9   8   7   6   '5

LifeWay
CHRISTIAN STORES®

****

Lifeway Christian Stores
Store #9235
20230 Katy Freeway
Katy, TX, 77449
281-829-2200

****

Customer #: 050072135

ITEM	QTY	PRICE	TOTAL
0012933355	1	$7.99	$7.99

HEAVEN STUDY GUIDE PB

Sub Total $7.99
Tax @ $0.66

Total $8.65
Cash $20.00
CHANGE <====> $-11.35

Sales Associate: 188

Lifeway Christian Stores
Thanks for shopping with us!
Be sure to visit our web site:
www.lifewaystores.com

Trx 7046 Str 9235 Reg 001 3/30/11 4:32PM

Customer Copy

Refund & Exchange Policy

Biblical Solutions for Life

Merchandise presented for a return must be accompanied by the original LifeWay store receipt. The purchase price will be refunded in the method of original payment (cash, credit card, etc.). Items purchased by check may be returned for a refund after 14 business days.

Only products purchased from LifeWay may be returned. A merchandise credit may be issued for returns unaccompanied by the original LifeWay store receipt or other proof of purchase with management approval. The returned merchandise must be carried by LifeWay at the time of the return. Returns must be completed within 90 days of purchase and merchandise must be in saleable condition.

Software, music, and videos may be exchanged for same product if defective or refunded if the package has not been opened.

Other restrictions may apply. See store for details.

Refund & Exchange Policy

Biblical Solutions for Life

Merchandise presented for a return must be accompanied by the original LifeWay store receipt. The purchase price will be refunded in the method of original payment (cash, credit card, etc.). Items purchased by check may be returned for a refund after 14 business days.

Only products purchased from LifeWay may be returned. A merchandise credit may be issued for returns unaccompanied by the original LifeWay store receipt or other proof of purchase with management approval. The returned merchandise must be carried by LifeWay at the time of the return. Returns must be completed within 90 days of purchase and merchandise must be in saleable condition.

Software, music, and videos may be exchanged for same product if defective or refunded if the package has not been opened.

Other restrictions may apply. See store for details.

Refund & Exchange Policy

Biblical Solutions for Life

Merchandise presented for a return must be accompanied by the original LifeWay store receipt. The purchase price will be refunded in the method of original payment (cash, credit card, etc.). Items purchased by check may be returned for a refund after 14 business days.

Only products purchased from LifeWay may be returned. A merchandise credit may be issued for returns unaccompanied by the original LifeWay store receipt or other proof of purchase with management approval. The returned merchandise must be carried by LifeWay at the time of the return. Returns must be completed within 90 days of purchase and merchandise must be in saleable condition.

Software, music, and videos may be exchanged for same product if defective or refunded if the package has not been opened.

Other restrictions may apply. See store for details.

proof of purchase with management approval. The returned merchandise must be carried by LifeWay at the time of the return. Returns must be completed within 90 days of purchase and merchandise must be in saleable condition.

Software, music, and videos may be exchanged for same product if defective or refunded if the package has not been opened.

CONTENTS

PART I
A THEOLOGY OF HEAVEN

PART II
QUESTIONS AND ANSWERS ABOUT HEAVEN

SECTION TEN

WHAT WILL OUR RELATIONSHIPS BE LIKE?

SECTION ELEVEN

WHAT ABOUT ANIMALS?

SECTION TWELVE

WHAT WILL WE DO IN HEAVEN?

PART III
LIVING IN LIGHT OF HEAVEN

ACKNOWLEDGMENTS

I want to thank the following people:

Jennifer Leo, who did some early work developing study questions;

*Sandi Swanson, who graciously volunteered her time
and made some important additions;*

Dave Lindstedt for his fine editing;

Carol Traver and Travis Thrasher for doing . . . whatever it is they do;

Bonnie Hiestand for typing in my revisions;

Kathy Norquist for helping me with this and everything else;

Nanci Alcorn for cheerfully freeing me to work on this and other projects;

*My grandchildren
—Jake Stump, Matthew Franklin, Tyler Stump, and Jack Franklin—
whose names I just felt like mentioning;*

*Jesus Christ, who paid our way to Heaven and by his grace is preparing
that fantastic place for us.*

HOW TO GET THE MOST FROM YOUR STUDY OF *HEAVEN*

The questions in this study guide are intended to facilitate group discussion and your personal study. When significant issues and statements in each chapter catch your eye, jot down a Scripture passage, quotation, or page number from the book related to something that you've underlined or wish to discuss. Use Scripture as often as possible, including passages you think of and those cited in *Heaven.* This will help to center your study on God's Word.

In preparation for your study of *Heaven,* read Revelation 21–22 at least three times, using a couple of different Bible translations, if possible. (You might want to write down some observations and questions as you go.) This will whet your appetite for Heaven, and especially for the New Earth! When you're done reading the book, you'll have a much deeper understanding and appreciation of Revelation 21–22 and other passages.

A note about the revised edition of *Heaven*

In the preface to *Heaven,* I invited readers to contact me if they believed they had biblical grounds for disagreeing with anything in the book. I was—and still am—open to correction, and I promised to make any warranted changes in future editions. During the first two years of the book's publication, I received a lot of good feedback and many questions asking for clarification of various points. I am grateful for these questions and criticisms. By mid-2006, I had received enough feedback on certain issues to warrant a modest revision of the book. This revised edition was published in September 2006. Several of the changes caused the pagination of the revised edition to change. Because we make reference in the *Heaven Study Guide* to specific pages in *Heaven*, the revision also necessitated a change in these page number references. In this study guide, therefore, you will occasionally see two sets of page number references (for example: "See *Heaven*, p. 149, or p. 155 in revised edition"). These references will help you find the specific pages in *Heaven* that pertain to the questions in the study guide.

How to tell if you have the revised edition of *Heaven*

Look at the copyright page in *Heaven* (on the reverse side of the title page). In the bottom left-hand corner, under the line that reads, "Printed in the United States of America," you will see two lines of numbers. On the bottom line, if the number farthest to the right is 9 or lower, you have the first edition. If that number is 10 or above, you have the revised edition.

Preface and Introduction:
The Subject of Heaven

Because of our wrong assumptions about the eternal state, we bring misguided perspectives to what it will mean to see God or be with him. We succumb to the vague, ethereal notions of eastern religions rather than build our understanding on the concrete, physical depictions of biblical and historical Christianity. We fail to envision God as forever incarnate in the risen Christ, and we fail to recognize the New Earth as a physical environment, civilization, and culture in which God will dwell with us.

1. What are you looking forward to in your study of Heaven?

_____

_____

_____

_____

2. Read Acts 17:11. What does this passage say, and how does it relate to how we should view claims about the afterlife based on near-death experiences and personal speculation?

_____

_____

_____

_____

3. Consider 1 Thessalonians 5:21: "Test everything. Hold on to the good." How should this principle be applied to reading any book other than the Bible, including *Heaven*?

_____

_____

_____

_____

4. "The sense that we will live forever *somewhere* has shaped every civilization in human history. . . . Anthropological evidence suggests that every culture has a God-given, innate sense of the eternal—that this world is not all there is" (*Heaven, xix*, or *xvii* in revised edition). Do you think this statement is significant or revealing? In what way?

_____

_____

_____

5. Read Psalm 39:4-5. How are these verses important as we consider the subject of Heaven?

_____

_____

_____

_____

6. Ancient merchants often wrote the words *memento mori*—"think of death"—in large letters on the first page of their accounting books. What perspective did this bring to their daily lives? Is anticipating death unhealthy, or can it be healthy?

_____

_____

_____

7. What did you learn from the story of Florence Chadwick, the swimmer? How does this story relate to the subject of Heaven?

_____

_____

_____

_____

PART I
A THEOLOGY OF HEAVEN

CHAPTER 1
Are You Looking Forward to Heaven?

In *The Adventures of Huckleberry Finn*, . . . Miss Watson takes a dim view of Huck's fun-loving spirit. According to Huck, "She went on and told me all about the good place. She said all a body would have to do there was go around all day long with a harp and sing, forever and ever. So I didn't think much of it. . . . I asked her if she reckoned Tom Sawyer would go there, and she said not by a considerable sight. I was glad about that, because I wanted him and me to be together."

1. As you begin reading the book, what do you already believe about Heaven?

_____

_____

_____

_____

2. What do you remember learning about Heaven as you were growing up? Who or what were your sources of information?

_____

_____

_____

_____

_____

3. "What God made us to desire . . . is exactly what he promises to those who follow Jesus Christ: a resurrected life in a resurrected body, with the resurrected Christ on a resurrected Earth" (*Heaven*, p. 7). How does this concept of Heaven compare with yours?

_____

_____

_____

_____

_____

4. Discuss how Heaven has "fallen off our radar screens" as a culture. Why don't we think more about it?

_____

_____

_____

_____

5. Read John 8:44 and Revelation 13:6 in the NIV. What role does Satan play in keeping us from anticipating Heaven?

_____

_____

_____

6. Review "Resisting Naturalism's Spell" at the end of chapter 1 (see *Heaven*, pp. 12–13). What is naturalism, and why should we resist it? *How* can we resist it?

_____

_____

_____

CHAPTER 2
Is Heaven Beyond Our Imagination?

The writers of Scripture present Heaven in many ways, including as a garden, a city, and a kingdom. Because gardens, cities, and kingdoms are familiar to us, they afford us a bridge to understanding Heaven. However, many people make the mistake of assuming that these are *merely* analogies with no actual correspondence to the reality of Heaven. . . . Too often we've been taught that Heaven is a non-physical realm, which cannot have real gardens, cities, kingdoms, buildings, banquets, or bodies. So we fail to take seriously what Scripture tells us about Heaven as a familiar, physical, tangible *place*.

1. God has given each of us an imagination and expects us to use it. Why do you think that many Christians shy away from studying Scripture and letting it guide their imagination to visualize what Heaven will be like?

_____

_____

_____

2. Describe a place you've visited or an experience you've had that helps you envision what some aspect of Heaven will be like.

_____

_____

_____

_____

3. What does 1 Corinthians 2:9-10 tell us? This passage isn't about Heaven in any direct sense. But even if it can be applied to Heaven, how does its real meaning differ from the way it is typically understood?

_____

_____

_____

_____

4. In Colossians 3:1-2, what are we commanded to do? How can we do this in our daily lives?

_____

_____

_____

5. Why is it appropriate—and biblical—to involve all our physical senses when imagining Heaven?

_____

_____

_____

CHAPTER 3
Is Heaven Our Default Destination . . . or Is Hell?

The great danger is that we will *assume* we are headed for Heaven. Judging by what's said at most funerals, you'd think nearly *everyone's* going to Heaven, wouldn't you? But Jesus made it clear that most people are *not* going to Heaven: "Small is the gate and narrow the road that leads to life, and only a few find it" (Matthew 7:14).

1. "For every American who believes he's going to Hell, there are 120 who believe they're going to Heaven" (*Heaven*, p. 23). How do Christ's words in Matthew 7:13-14 relate to this statement?

_____

_____

2. How does our society's incorrect thinking about our "default destination" affect our motivation to preach the truth about sin and God's gift of redemption?

_____

_____

3. Where do we as a culture receive our information about Hell? What are some of the stereotypical depictions you've heard or seen?

_____

_____

_____

4. Read Matthew 5:21-30; 10:28; and Mark 9:43-48. According to Jesus, what is Hell like?

_____

_____

_____

_____

_____

5. Many people believe it is unloving to talk to others about Hell, yet Jesus talked more about Hell than anyone else in the Bible did. Why is this significant?

_____

_____

_____

_____

6. Read Mark 8:34-38. What haunting questions did Jesus ask? How does this motivate you to share the truth about sin, redemption, Heaven, and Hell?

_____

_____

_____

7. Explain how talking honestly about both Heaven and Hell expresses love for your family and friends. Is there someone you need to talk to about the only two possible eternal destinations?

_____

_____

_____

_____

CHAPTER 4
Can You Know You're Going to Heaven?

Throughout the ages, countless people have been too busy to respond to Christ's invitation to his wedding banquet. Many assume that the good they've done—perhaps attending church, being baptized, singing in the choir, or helping in a soup kitchen—will be enough to gain entry to Heaven. But people who do not respond to Christ's invitation to forgive their sins are people whose names aren't written in the Lamb's Book of Life.

1. In what ways does our culture reinforce the mistaken idea that everyone is going to Heaven?

_____

_____

_____

_____

_____

2. What are some of the reasons you've heard for why people deserve to go to Heaven? Will any of these things get them into Heaven?

_____

_____

_____

_____

_____

3. What did you learn from the story of the wedding singer whose name wasn't written in the guest book and who therefore couldn't enter the wedding reception?

_____

_____

_____

_____

4. Various passages of Scripture show that there is only one way to enter Heaven. List a few of those passages (including John 14:6 and Acts 4:12) and discuss what they say.

_____

_____

_____

5. Do you know for sure that you're going to Heaven? Why or why not?

_____

_____

_____

6. How would you respond to people who say they believe in Jesus Christ but don't need to be part of a church?

_____

_____

_____

7. How do your attitudes and perspectives about life on Earth affect your understanding and anticipation of life in Heaven?

_____

_____

_____

CHAPTER 5
What Is the Nature of the Present Heaven?

When we die, believers in Christ will not go to the Heaven where we'll live forever. Instead, we'll go to an intermediate Heaven. In that Heaven—where those who died covered by Christ's blood are now—we'll await the time of Christ's return to the earth, our bodily resurrection, the final judgment, and the creation of the new heavens and New Earth. If we fail to grasp this truth, we will fail to understand the biblical doctrine of Heaven.

1. What do you think of the concept that there is an intermediate Heaven where we live between our death and resurrection, a concept that theologians have long taught? Is this a new thought to you? (Remember, this intermediate Heaven is not purgatory; it is simply where believers who die live until the final resurrection.)

_____

_____

_____

_____

_____

2. How does the present (intermediate) Heaven differ from the eternal Heaven?

_____

_____

_____

_____

3. What does Revelation 21:1-4 teach us about the New Earth? What is the particular significance of verse 3 as it relates to where Heaven (God's dwelling place) will be located?

_____

_____

_____

_____

_____

4. Where does the human spirit go at death? Cite Scripture to support your answer.

_____

_____

_____

_____

_____

5. What are the implications of God's coming down to live with us on the New Earth, as opposed to our going up to live forever in the spirit realm as disembodied beings?

_____

_____

_____

_____

6. Discuss the differences between the two types of judgment we will encounter after death. What is the result of the judgment of faith? What is the result of the judgment of works?

_____

_____

_____

_____

7. What do Stephen's vision of Heaven (Acts 7:55-56) and Gehazi's vision of the chariots of fire (2 Kings 6:17) tell us about the present Heaven?

_____

_____

_____

_____

_____

CHAPTER 6
Is the Present Heaven a Physical Place?

Though God chooses to dwell in Heaven, he does not need a dwelling place. However, as finite humans, we do. It's no problem for the all-powerful God, a spirit, to dwell in a spiritual realm or a physical realm or a realm that includes both. The real question is whether people, being by nature both spiritual and physical, can dwell in a realm without physical properties.

1. Discuss the implications of this quote from John Milton's *Paradise Lost:* "What if Earth be but the shadow of Heav'n, and things therein each to other like, more then on Earth is thought?"

_____

_____

_____

_____

_____

2. Although many think of the current Heaven as a completely non-physical place, there is considerable biblical evidence that it has physical properties. What is some of this evidence? What is your own viewpoint?

_____

_____

_____

_____

3. What is Christoplatonism (see *Heaven*, p. 52), and how does it apply to your view of Heaven, the final resurrection, and the New Earth? Have christoplatonic assumptions affected your own view of Heaven? (For further treatment of this subject, see *Heaven*, Appendix A.)

_____

_____

_____

_____

4. According to Scripture, what are some of the things that are similar in Heaven and on Earth? In the following Scripture passages—2 Kings 2:11; Hebrews 8:5; and Revelation 7:9; 8:6, 13; 15:8; 19:14—what suggests that Heaven could be a physical realm?

_____

_____

_____

5. The word *paradise* comes from the Persian word *pairidaeza*, meaning "a walled park" or "an enclosed garden." It is used to describe the great walled gardens of the Persian king Cyrus's royal palaces. The Greek word for *paradise* is used of the Garden of Eden, and it became the word to describe the eternal state of the righteous and even the present Heaven (Jesus spoke of Paradise and so did Paul). The tree of life from Genesis 1–2 is presently in Paradise (Revelation 2:7). In light of this, what does the use of the

word *paradise* to describe the present Heaven suggest about whether or not it has physical components?

_____

_____

_____

6. What do the depictions of people wearing clothes, holding palm branches, and walking and talking in the present Heaven imply about the possibility of our having physical forms in Heaven? What about Enoch, Elijah, and Moses, or Christ's story of the rich man and Lazarus?

_____

_____

_____

7. If we do have physical forms in the present Heaven, it is a temporary condition as we await the final resurrection (which will involve the reconstitution of our original bodies). Do you agree or disagree with this view?

_____

_____

_____

CHAPTER 7
What Is Life Like in the Present Heaven?

Memory is a basic element of personality. If we are truly *ourselves* in Heaven, there must be continuity of memory from Earth to Heaven. We will not be different people, but the same people marvelously relocated and transformed. Heaven cleanses us but does not revise or extinguish our origins or history. Undoubtedly we will remember God's works of grace in our lives that comforted, assured, sustained, and empowered us to live for him.

1. Review the list of characteristics of the present Heaven as described in Revelation 6 (summarized on pp. 65–67 of *Heaven*). Do these seem to be a fair understanding of what this Scripture really suggests? Are any of these points surprising to you? If so, which ones and why?

_____

_____

_____

2. What is the biblical evidence that, in Heaven, we will remember much or even most of our lives on Earth? Is that a comforting thought to you? Why or why not?

_____

_____

3. Why is it hard for us to picture people in the present Heaven seeing and praying for people on Earth? Would awareness of what's happening on Earth keep people in Heaven from being happy? Why or why not?

_____

_____

_____

4. What is the difference between happiness that is a result of ignorance and happiness that is a result of perspective? Which sort of happiness do you think people experience in Heaven?

_____

_____

_____

5. Does your understanding of life in the present Heaven affect your perspective of the "interruption" of your relationships with believing loved ones who have died? If so, in what ways?

_____

_____

_____

CHAPTER 8
This World Is Not Our Home . . . or Is It?

We long for a return to Paradise—a perfect world, without the corruption of sin, where God walks with us and talks with us in the cool of the day. Because we're human beings, we desire something tangible and physical, something that will not fade away. And that is exactly what God promises us—a home that will not be destroyed, a kingdom that will not fade, a city with unshakable foundations, an incorruptible inheritance.

1. Have you ever been homesick? What did it feel like? Because of our connection to Adam and Eve, can you see how we could be homesick for Eden? How might that emotion make us long for a New Earth?

_____

_____

_____

_____

2. How does our ability to imagine Heaven as a tangible place, with physical wonders and human relationships and activities, relate to our desire to go there?

_____

_____

_____

3. Study the chart of the three eras of mankind and Earth (see *Heaven*, pp. 82–85). Does it make sense to you? Does it raise any questions?

_____

_____

_____

4. How does understanding God's original plan for mankind and the earth help you to understand what God has planned for mankind and the earth in the future? In what ways can you see God's plan unfolding in our present day and age?

_____

_____

_____

5. Comparing Genesis 1–2 with Revelation 21–22, cite at least two examples of the perfect symmetry of God's plan.

_____

_____

_____

6. How does God's plan for resurrection and a New Earth demonstrate that "matter matters"?

_____

_____

_____

Why Is Earth's Redemption Essential to God's Plan?

God's Kingdom and dominion are not about what happens in some remote, unearthly place; instead, they are about what happens on the earth, which God created for his glory. . . . His glory is manifested in his creation. The earth is not disposable. It is essential to God's plan. God promises that ultimately the whole Earth will be filled with his glory.

1. Christians talk a lot about being "made new" in Christ. Chapter 9 talks about being restored to God's original design (back to the way humanity was before the corruption of sin and the Curse). Is this a different perspective on being "made new" than you have previously considered? In what ways?

_____

_____

_____

_____

2. List some of the *re-* words used in Scripture to describe God's plan for mankind and the earth. How do these words help to shape your understanding of the three phases of Earth's history?

_____

_____

_____

_____

3. Because we know that our bodies will be destroyed by decay after death, yet God will raise them into new bodies, does it make sense that though the earth will be destroyed, God will raise it into a New Earth? Is this a different idea for you?

_____

_____

_____

_____

4. A *new* car is still a *car*, not a non-car, even if it has many new and different features. How does this same idea apply to our understanding of the New Earth and our new bodies? (Will the earth still be Earth? Will our bodies still be bodies?)

_____

_____

_____

_____

5. Compare Isaiah 60; 65:17-25; and Ezekiel 47 with Revelation 21–22. Although some statements in the Old Testament passages may apply to the old Earth, which is still under the Curse—or perhaps to the earth during the Millennium—some clearly speak of the New Earth. What do these passages suggest about life on the New Earth?

_____

_____

_____

_____

CHAPTER 10
What Will It Mean for the Curse to Be Lifted?

We have never seen the earth as God made it. Our planet as we know it is a shadowy, halftone image of the original. But it does whet our appetites for the New Earth, doesn't it? If the present Earth, so diminished by the Curse, is at times so beautiful and wonderful; if our bodies, so diminished by the Curse, are at times overcome with a sense of the earth's beauty and wonder; then how magnificent will the New Earth be?

1. Revelation 22:3 tells us that on the New Earth there will no longer be any Curse. Imagine what life will be like when the Curse is lifted. What will change? What will remain the same?

_____

_____

_____

2. How can resurrection succeed in reversing the Curse, whereas permanently annihilating the world could not?

_____

_____

_____

3. What is Christ's role as the "last Adam"? How will Christ fulfill that role as he occupies the throne in the New Jerusalem on the New Earth?

_____

_____

_____

4. Describe the "already and not yet" paradox that characterizes life on the present Earth. How does this paradox affect our lives today? What will be different when this paradox is resolved on the New Earth?

_____

_____

_____

5. In addition to rescuing human souls from ultimate destruction, for what other reason did Jesus come to Earth? (See *Heaven*, p. 106, or p. 107 in revised edition.)

_____

_____

_____

SECTION FOUR: ANTICIPATING RESURRECTION

CHAPTER 11
Why Is Resurrection So Important?

The physical resurrection of Jesus Christ is the cornerstone of redemption—both for mankind and for the earth. Indeed, without Christ's resurrection and what it means—an eternal future for fully restored human beings dwelling on a fully restored Earth—there is no Christianity.

1. According to the apostle Paul (1 Corinthians 15:12-28), why is resurrection so important?

_____

_____

_____

2. Why is a "spiritual" or "non-physical" resurrection a contradiction in terms?

_____

_____

_____

_____

3. What factors make it difficult for some people to accept the idea of bodily resurrection?

_____

_____

_____

_____

4. The principle of "redemptive continuity" says that God will not scrap his original creation and start over. Instead, God will take his fallen, corrupted children and restore, refresh, and renew them to their original design; and he will do the same for Earth (see *Heaven*, p. 112, or pp. 114–115 in revised edition). Why is "redemptive continuity" important to our understanding of the Heaven in which we'll live forever?

_____

_____

_____

_____

5. What will be some of the similarities and differences between our earthly bodies and our resurrected bodies? What Scripture passages support your answer?

_____

_____

_____

_____

CHAPTER 12
Why Does All Creation Await Our Resurrection?

The fallen but redeemed children of God will be transformed into something new: sinless, wise stewards of the earth. Today the earth is dying; but before it dies—or in its death—it will give birth to the New Earth. The New Earth will be the child of the old Earth, just as the new human race will be the children of the old race. Yet it is still *us*, the same human beings, and it will also be the same Earth.

1. In what ways has God built the promise of resurrection into the fabric of nature? What can we learn from observing the seasons? the water cycle? other natural systems?

_____

_____

_____

2. What is the central teaching of Romans 8:18-25? How does this affect your view of the concept of a coming New Earth and what we might expect to find there?

_____

_____

_____

3. Have you ever thought about Christ's resurrection as affecting *all* of creation—not just human beings? How does this truth affect your view of Heaven?

_____

_____

_____

4. Discuss Paul's use of childbirth imagery (as opposed to death imagery) to describe the end of the world. What implications does it have for what "the end of the world" really means?

_____

_____

_____

_____

CHAPTER 13
How Far-Reaching Is the Resurrection?

It's hard for us to think accurately about the New Earth because we're so accustomed to speaking of Heaven as the opposite of Earth. . . . Because ethereal notions of Heaven have largely gone unchallenged, we often think of Heaven as less real and less substantial than life here and now. . . . But in Heaven . . . we'll be fully alive and fully physical in a fully physical universe.

1. Paul writes in 1 Corinthians 15:58, "Always give yourselves fully to the work of the Lord, because you know that your labor in the Lord is not in vain." In the context of 1 Corinthians 15, *why* is our labor not in vain?

_____

_____

_____

_____

2. How should the prospect that the quality of our work on Earth will be tested by fire affect our outlook on Heaven, our perspective on life, and our deeds in this lifetime?

_____

_____

_____

_____

3. What is erroneous in the following statement made by a Christian father about his Christian son who had died: "That's the last time I'll ever see him in his body"?

_____

_____

_____

_____

4. When we think of God "saving souls," how does this underestimate the extent of God's redemption? What else does God save besides our souls?

_____

_____

_____

_____

5. Review the description of Heaven from the novel *Safely Home,* cited on pp. 131–133 of *Heaven* (p. 135 of revised edition). Does this description match your concept of Heaven? How is it different?

_____

_____

_____

_____

CHAPTER 14
Where and When Will Our Deliverance Come?

When Jesus spoke to his disciples before ascending to Heaven, he said it was not for them to know *when* he would restore God's Kingdom on Earth (Acts 1:6-8), but he did not say they wouldn't know *if* he would restore God's Kingdom. After all, restoring the Kingdom of God on Earth was his ultimate mission.

1. Explain your understanding of the following statement: "In the end it will be a far greater world, even for having gone through the birth pains of suffering and sin—yes, *even sin*. The New Earth will justify the old Earth's disaster, make good out of it, putting it in perspective. It will preserve and perpetuate Earth's original design and heritage" (*Heaven*, p. 137, or p. 143 in revised edition). Do you agree or disagree? Why?

_____

_____

_____

_____

2. What are some of the things the Old Testament teaches us about Heaven? Consider especially the promises concerning land (*erets*, the Hebrew word for Earth), animals, and Jerusalem at peace. Why are we sometimes slow to recognize these promises?

_____

_____

_____

3. Read Revelation 20 and note the six references to the Millennium, the thousand-year reign of Christ. What are the three major differing viewpoints concerning the Millennium? Which position makes the most sense to you?

_____

_____

_____

4. Can those who disagree about the Millennium agree about the New Earth? Why or why not?

_____

_____

_____

CHAPTER 15

Will the Old Earth Be Destroyed . . . or Renewed?

The earth's death will be no more final than our own. The destruction of the old Earth in God's purifying judgment will immediately be followed by its resurrection to new life. Earth's fiery "end" will open straight into a glorious new beginning. . . . It will just keep getting better and better.

1. Discuss both the destructive and the purifying qualities of fire. How do these images help us think about how the present Earth will come to an end?

_____

_____

_____

2. How might the transformation of a caterpillar into a butterfly illustrate God's plan for renewing the earth? What insight does it offer to your understanding of becoming "a new creation" (2 Corinthians 5:17)?

_____

_____

_____

_____

3. What evidence does the Bible offer to support the idea of a temporary—not permanent—destruction of the earth? Consider 2 Peter 3:5-13, noting especially how the earth was "destroyed" by water in the Flood, yet still continued to exist. If the surface of the earth is scorched and purified, would that qualify as destruction?

_____

_____

_____

_____

4. Even if Earth is utterly obliterated and its atoms scattered, would it be any harder for God to restore it as a New Earth than to restore millions of decomposed bodies, many of which died thousands of years ago?

_____

_____

_____

_____

5. In Revelation 21:1, what does *new* mean in the context of a New Heaven and New Earth? (See *Heaven,* p. 149, or p. 155 in revised edition.)

_____

_____

_____

CHAPTER 16

Will the New Earth
Be Familiar . . . like Home?

Sometimes when we look at this world's breathtaking beauty—standing in a gorgeous place where the trees and flowers and rivers and mountains are wondrous—we feel a twinge of disappointment. Why? Because we know we're going to leave this behind. . . . What we really want is to live forever in a world with all the beauty and none of the ugliness—a world without sin, death, the Curse, and all the personal and relational problems and disappointments they create.

1. Do you think Christians sometimes speak of God's original work on Earth, and his plan for people to rule the earth, as if he somehow failed? Have Satan and fallen humans messed up God's plan, so that righteous, embodied people will never rule a totally righteous and sinless Earth?

_____

_____

_____

_____

2. Review the list, found on p. 155 of _Heaven_ (p. 161 in revised edition), of what the Bible says about Heaven. Which of these are familiar, and which are new ideas to you?

_____

_____

_____

_____

3. What qualities of "home" will we discover in Heaven? Are these thoughts comforting to you?

_____

_____

_____

_____

_____

4. Why is it significant that the world to come is called a *New* Earth (rather than a *non*-Earth)?

_____

_____

_____

_____

5. Discuss your response to the following statement: "Because Heaven is God's dwelling place, it is inappropriate to think of the eternal Heaven in earthly terms." Do you agree or disagree? Explain.

_____

_____

_____

_____

6. Discuss why it is partially accurate yet also partially inaccurate for Christians to say, "This earth is not my home." How would you reword the sentence so that it is fully accurate?

_____

_____

_____

_____

CHAPTER 17
What Will It Mean to See God?

God is the one we really long for. His presence brings satisfaction; his absence brings thirst and longing. *Our longing for Heaven is a longing for God*—a longing that involves not only our inner beings, but our bodies as well. Being with God is the heart and soul of Heaven. Every other heavenly pleasure will derive from and be secondary to his presence. God's greatest gift to us is, and always will be, himself.

1. Revelation 22:4 promises us that we will see God's face on the New Earth. Why is this an astounding statement?

_____

_____

_____

2. What do you think it will mean to see God face-to-face?

_____

_____

_____

3. What is the essence of eternal life according to John 17:3? How should this truth motivate the way we live day to day?

_____

_____

_____

4. We need not wait until the New Earth to catch glimpses of God. Romans 1:20 tells us that "since the creation of the world God's invisible qualities . . . have been clearly seen, being understood from what has been made." What has God created that shows some of his qualities? (Use specific examples.) What are some of God's "invisible qualities" that we can clearly see on Earth today?

_____

_____

_____

5. Refer to p. 172 of *Heaven* (p. 178 in revised edition). What is the lesson to be learned from the movie *Babette's Feast*? (It might be worth renting this full-length movie and watching it together as a family or group.)

_____

_____

_____

6. How does reminding ourselves that God made the earth, that he desires for us to enjoy it, and that he intends for us to live on the New Earth help us to appreciate our present lives?

_____

_____

_____

CHAPTER 18

What Will It Mean for God to Dwell Among Us?

The marriage of the God of Heaven with the people of Earth will also bring the marriage of Heaven and Earth. There will not be two universes—one the primary home of God and angels, the other the primary home of humanity. Nothing will separate us from God, and nothing will separate Earth and Heaven. Once God and mankind dwell together, there will be no difference between Heaven and Earth.

1. If you have read the best-selling novel *The Five People You Meet in Heaven* or have seen the made-for-TV movie based on the book, explain the ways it is accurate or inaccurate in how it portrays Heaven. (See *Heaven*, p. 179, or p. 185 in revised edition.)

_____

_____

_____

2. How does Satan interfere with our ability to envision Heaven? What does he stand to gain from our misconceptions?

_____

_____

_____

3. Read John 14:3; 2 Corinthians 5:8; and Philippians 1:23. What is the common thread? What do you think it will be like to be inseparable from Jesus?

_____

_____

_____

4. What do you think of the idea that in Heaven God will serve us? What scriptural basis is there for believing this? In what ways do you think he might serve us?

_____

_____

_____

_____

5. Can you envision what it will mean to rest and relax in Heaven? What will it mean to be happy, content, worry free, and without fear of what will happen next or what we or others will do?

_____

_____

_____

CHAPTER 19
How Will We Worship God?

Today, many Christians have come to depreciate or ignore the beatific vision, supposing that beholding God would be of mere passing interest, becoming monotonous over time. But those who know God know that he is anything but boring. Seeing God will be dynamic, not static. It will mean exploring new beauties, unfolding new mysteries—forever. We'll explore God's being, an experience delightful beyond comprehension.

1. Describe some of the best worship you've ever experienced. What was it like? How did it give you a taste of what worship will be like in Heaven?

_____

_____

_____

2. How does Revelation 5:11-14 depict worship?

_____

_____

_____

3. What word picture represents the righteous/faithful acts of the saints (Revelation 19:8), and how does it motivate you to live for Christ? (See *Heaven*, pp. 191–192, or pp. 199–200 in revised edition.)

_____

_____

_____

_____

4. Read Hebrews 10:25. Why does properly preparing for Heaven involve being part of the church now? (See *Heaven*, p. 193, or pp. 200–201 in revised edition.)

_____

_____

_____

5. What are the main reasons for celebrating in Heaven?

_____

_____

_____

6. Discuss the following statement: "Longing for Heaven is longing for God, and longing for God is longing for Heaven." God and Heaven are not the same. Yet in some sense they are inseparable. Why is this so?

_____

_____

_____

CHAPTER 20
What Does God's Eternal Kingdom Involve?

We've been born into the family of an incredibly wealthy landowner. There's not a millimeter of cosmic geography that doesn't belong to him, and by extension to his children, his heirs. Our Father has a family business that stretches across the whole universe. He entrusts to us management of the family business, and that's what we'll do for eternity: manage God's assets and rule his universe, representing him as his image-bearers, children, and ambassadors.

1. Discuss the differences between "earthly" things and "worldly" things. How would you distinguish between them based on Scripture?

_____

_____

_____

_____

_____

2. Read Revelation 5:1-14 and imagine yourself in the throne room as God the Father holds the sealed scroll. Describe what you think it will be like when the Lamb steps forward to take the scroll.

_____

_____

_____

_____

3. Read Genesis 12:1-7. What is the significance of "land" in God's eternal Kingdom?

_____

_____

_____

_____

_____

4. When God made a covenant with Abraham, what did he promise to Abraham first?

_____

_____

_____

_____

_____

5. According to Ephesians 1:10, what is God's plan for the new heavens and New Earth?

_____

_____

_____

_____

6. With what you've learned about a transformed Earth and Kingdom, how has your picture of Heaven changed? Does this increase your motivation to live every day for the King?

_____

_____

_____

_____

_____

CHAPTER 21
Will We Actually Rule with Christ?

Imagine responsibility, service, and leadership that is pure joy. The responsibility that God will entrust to us as a reward can only be good for us, and we'll find delight in it. To rule on the New Earth will be to enable, equip, and guide, offering wisdom and encouragement to those under our authority.

1. Read Zechariah 9:9-10 and discuss the twofold prophecy. When was the first part fulfilled? When will the second part be fulfilled?

_____

_____

_____

_____

2. Who are Christ's co-heirs? What do heirs inherit?

_____

_____

_____

_____

3. Who will rule the earth with Jesus Christ? What might this ruling entail?

_____

_____

_____

_____

4. What do you think about the idea of being a ruler of the earth? Can you see yourself in this role? Why is this idea hard to grasp?

_____

_____

_____

_____

5. What if we don't like the idea of ruling and we think we would rather not do it? (How might God respond to our reluctance? What would he say to us?)

_____

_____

_____

_____

6. Through the challenges you now face, what dreams might God be preparing for you to live out on the New Earth?

_____

_____

_____

_____

CHAPTER 22
How Will We Rule God's Kingdom?

Earth exists for the same reason that mankind and everything else exists: to glorify God. God is glorified when we take our rightful, intended place in his creation and exercise the dominion that he bestowed on us. . . . God's intention for humans was that we would occupy the whole Earth and reign over it. This dominion would produce God-exalting societies in which we would exercise the creativity, imagination, intellect, and skills befitting beings created in God's image, thereby manifesting his attributes.

1. What is God's purpose for human beings? How does Genesis 1:26-28 help to answer this? (See *Heaven*, p. 218, or p. 226 in revised edition.)

_____

_____

_____

_____

2. We must be clear about what Scripture is saying when it refers to this world in a negative way. For example, our understanding of James 4:4 can be enhanced by the addition of an implied phrase: "Friendship with the world *[as it is now, under the Curse]* is hatred toward God." What is the significance of the words that are in brackets? Do they accurately capture the meaning of the passage? What interpretive error do they keep us from committing? (See *Heaven*, pp. 219–220, or pp. 227–228 in revised edition.)

_____

_____

_____

_____

3. Review the discussion of Christ's ever-expanding government (see *Heaven*, pp. 224–225, or pp. 232–233 in revised edition). Which explanation makes the most sense to you? What do you think of the possibility that God will create new worlds in the future?

_____

_____

_____

4. How do our actions on the present Earth affect the role we will fulfill on the New Earth?

_____

_____

_____

_____

5. How will ruling—and being ruled—on the New Earth differ from those experiences on the present Earth? What will account for these differences?

_____

_____

_____

_____

PART II
QUESTIONS AND ANSWERS ABOUT HEAVEN

CHAPTER 23
Will the New Earth Be an Edenic Paradise?

Some people assume that the New Earth will "start over" with Eden's original paradise. However, Scripture demonstrates otherwise. The New Earth, as we've seen, includes a carryover of culture and nations. History won't start over with the New Earth any more than history started over when Adam and Eve were banished from the Garden. Eden was part of history. There was direct continuity from the pre-Fall world to the post-Fall world. Similarly, there will be direct continuity between the dying old Earth and the resurrected New Earth. The earthshaking Fall divided history, but it didn't end history. The resurrection of all things will divide Earth's history, but it won't end it.

1. Compare Eden, the present Earth, and the New Earth. What are some of the differences? What are the similarities?

_____

_____

2. Read Exodus 28:9-12. What is the significance of the onyx memorial stones on the priests' garments? (See also Genesis 2:11-12; Ezekiel 28:13; and Revelation 21:19-20.)

_____

_____

_____

_____

3. What portions or aspects of the old Earth do you hope will be found on the New Earth?

_____

_____

_____

_____

4. Based on Revelation 22:1-5, what type of place will the New Earth be?

_____

_____

_____

CHAPTER 24
What Is the New Jerusalem?

Everyone knows what a city is—a place with buildings, streets, and residences occupied by people and subject to a common government. Cities have inhabitants, visitors, bustling activity, cultural events, and gatherings involving music, the arts, education, religion, entertainment, and athletics. If the capital city of the New Earth doesn't have these defining characteristics of a city, it would seem misleading for Scripture to repeatedly call it a city.

1. Discuss the evidence that the New Jerusalem will be an actual city. What will it have in common with the present world's capital cities? What will be different?

_____

_____

_____

_____

2. Review the discussion on pp. 243–244 of *Heaven* (pp. 251–252 in revised edition). What is the significance of the gates of the New Jerusalem?

_____

_____

_____

_____

3. According to Philippians 3:20, where is a believer's citizenship *now*, and why is that important?

_____

_____

_____

_____

4. Will our enjoyment of the New Jerusalem depend on whether or not we presently enjoy city life on this earth? Why or why not?

_____

_____

_____

_____

CHAPTER 25

What Will the Great City Be Like?

The first place we may wish to explore will be the largest city that has ever existed—the capital city of the New Earth. The New Jerusalem will be a place of extravagant beauty and natural wonders. It will be a vast Eden, integrated with the best of human culture, under the reign of Christ. More wealth than has been accumulated in all human history will be spread freely across this immense city.

1. Which details of the New Jerusalem especially appeal to you?

_____

_____

_____

2. What do the elements of the New Jerusalem suggest about the kind of life resurrected people will live there?

_____

_____

_____

3. The tree of life that was in Eden (Genesis 1–3) is currently in the present Heaven (Revelation 2:7), yet it will be in the center of the New Jerusalem on the New Earth (Revelation 22:2). What is the tree of life, and what will it mean for us to eat its abundant and varied fruit?

_____

_____

_____

4. People debate about how big the New Jerusalem will really be. As you consider what is said in Revelation 21, what do you think the answer is, and why?

_____

_____

_____

_____

5. Why is it significant that there is no mention of a tree of the knowledge of good and evil to test us, as there was in Eden? (See *Heaven*, p. 249, or p. 257 in revised edition.)

_____

_____

_____

_____

_____

CHAPTER 26
Will There Be Space and Time?

We are finite physical creatures, and that means we must live in space and time. Where else would we live? Eden was in space and time, and the New Earth will be in space and time. . . . People imagine they're making Heaven sound wondrous when they say there's no space and time there. In fact, they make Heaven sound utterly alien and unappealing. We don't want to live in a realm—in fact, it couldn't even *be* a realm—that's devoid of space and time any more than a fish wants to live in a realm without water.

1. What does the forming of the new heavens suggest about the future of planets, stars, and deep-space elements of the present cosmos?

_____

_____

_____

_____

2. Read Mark 13:27 and Luke 24:39. What do these verses indicate about the spatial aspect of Heaven?

_____

_____

_____

_____

3. Is there any biblical evidence that space and time will be non-existent or different in Heaven? (What about the phrase "time shall be no more"?) Here are some verses to help you answer: Genesis 8:22; Isaiah 66:22-23; Luke 15:7; Ephesians 2:7; Revelation 4:10; 5:9-12; 6:10-11; 7:15; 8:1; and 22:2. (See *Heaven,* pp. 259–260, or pp. 266–268 in revised edition.)

_____

_____

_____

_____

4. "Buddhism, which knows no resurrection, teaches that time will be extinguished. Christianity, solidly based on a resurrection of cosmic dimensions, teaches that time will go on forever" (*Heaven,* p. 261, or p. 269 in revised edition). Do you agree or disagree? Why?

_____

_____

_____

CHAPTER 27
Will the New Earth Have Sun, Moon, Oceans, and Weather?

There will be direct continuity between this earth and the New Earth. But the Bible includes some passages that have led people to believe that the New Earth will have no sun, no moon, and no seas. . . . None of these verses actually says there will be no more sun or moon. They say that the New Jerusalem will not *need* their light, for sun and moon will be outshone by God's glory.

1. Read Revelation 21:23 and 22:5. What do these verses tell us about the sun, the moon, and the New Earth?

_____

_____

_____

_____

2. Revelation 21:1 says that on the New Earth "there was no longer any sea." Ezekiel 47:6-12, which mentions several things that are applied to the New Earth in Revelation 22, refers to the sea and to the river's waters making the sea fresh. Isaiah 60:5, 9, in another context that includes references to the New Earth, also makes reference to the sea. Based on the discussion in *Heaven,* pp. 265–267 (pp. 273–275 in revised edition), what do you conclude about the probable presence or absence of oceans on the New Earth? If there are no saltwater seas, could there still be large bodies of fresh water?

_____

_____

_____

_____

3. Will there be weather and seasons on the New Earth? How would you justify your answer based on Scripture and logic? (See *Heaven*, pp. 267–268, or pp. 275–277 in revised edition, for some ideas.)

_____

_____

_____

_____

4. It is possible to err on the side of assuming either that life will be very much the same on the New Earth or that it will be utterly different. Why do you think most Christians err on the side they do? Is a middle-ground approach helpful?

_____

_____

_____

_____

SECTION NINE: WHAT WILL OUR LIVES BE LIKE?

CHAPTER 28
Will We Be Ourselves?

Just as our genetic code and fingerprints are unique now, we should expect the same of our new bodies. Individual identity is an essential aspect of personhood. God is the creator of individual identities and personalities. He makes no two snowflakes, much less two people, alike. Not even "identical twins" are identical. Individuality preceded sin and the Curse. Individuality was God's plan from the beginning.

1. Discuss the differences between disembodied spirits and resurrected people. Are these differences important? Why?

_____

_____

_____

_____

2. In Heaven, will humans have emotions? Why do you think so? (See Luke 6:21; Revelation 6:10; 7:10; and 21:4.)

_____

_____

_____

_____

3. "We'll have many desires in Heaven, but they won't be *unholy* desires. Everything we want will be good" (*Heaven*, p. 277, or p. 285 in revised edition). What are some desires of your heart now that you hope to fulfill in Heaven?

_____

_____

_____

_____

4. How do you feel about being yourself (i.e., maintaining your own identity) in Heaven? Is that a relief, or does it make you uneasy? (Do you look forward to being yourself, but without all the bad parts?)

_____

_____

_____

_____

5. Read Isaiah 62:2; 65:15; Revelation 2:17; 3:12; 20:15; and 21:27. Do you think you might keep your own name as well as receive a new name in Heaven? Why?

_____

_____

_____

CHAPTER 29
What Will Our Bodies Be Like?

Our resurrection bodies will be free of the curse of sin, redeemed, and restored to their original beauty and purpose that goes back to Eden. The only bodies we've ever known are weak and diseased remnants of the original bodies God made for humans. But the bodies we'll have on the New Earth, in our resurrection, will be even more glorious than those of Adam and Eve.

1. Is it good news or bad news to you that you will have a body in eternity? What do you imagine it will be like?

_____

_____

_____

2. What are the bodily senses and qualities that you are most looking forward to exercising as a resurrected person on the New Earth? What aspects of your present body are you most looking forward to being different?

_____

_____

_____

3. Read Romans 8:17-18; 2 Corinthians 4:17; and 1 Peter 5:1-4. What prepares us to participate in God's glory?

_____

_____

_____

_____

4. Certainly, God could resurrect our bodies to any stage of life he chooses. But based on the discussion on pp. 288–290 of *Heaven* (pp. 297–299 in revised edition), which do you think is the most likely possibility: that we'll be resurrected to the age we were at death (or at the Second Coming), that we'll be resurrected to an ideal age (such as thirty or thirty-three), or that we'll appear ageless? Explain your answer.

_____

_____

_____

_____

CHAPTER 30
Will We Eat and Drink on the New Earth?

Words describing eating, meals, and food appear more than a thousand times in Scripture, and the English translation "feast" occurs another 187 times. Feasting involves celebration and fun, and it is profoundly relational. Great conversation, storytelling, relationship building, and laughter often happen during mealtimes. Feasts, including Passover, were spiritual gatherings that drew direct attention to God, his greatness, and his redemptive purposes.

1. What biblical evidence is there that we will eat and drink as resurrected beings on the New Earth?

_____

_____

_____

_____

2. Romans 14:17 says, "The kingdom of God is not a matter of eating and drinking, but of righteousness, peace and joy in the Holy Spirit." In context, is this passage saying we won't eat or drink on the New Earth? What *is* it saying?

_____

_____

_____

_____

3. Another passage cited to argue against eating and drinking in Heaven is 1 Corinthians 6:13 (NLT): "You say, 'Food is for the stomach, and the stomach is for food.' This is true, though someday God will do away with both of them." What is this passage actually saying, in context? (See *Heaven*, p. 294, or p. 304 in revised edition.)

_____

_____

_____

_____

4. Christ is said to have eaten with his disciples in his resurrection body. Why is that significant?

_____

_____

_____

5. According to Isaiah 25:6, who will prepare a banquet for us, and what will we enjoy together?

_____

_____

_____

6. Review the discussion on pp. 295–296 of *Heaven* (pp. 305–307 in revised edition) about eating meat in Heaven. Based on the evidence cited, do you believe that we'll be vegetarians, eat meat from dead animals, or eat meat provided by God in some other way? Explain your answer.

_____

_____

_____

CHAPTER 31
Will We Be Capable of Sinning?

Some people believe that if we have free will in Heaven, we'll have to be free to sin, as were the first humans. But Adam and Eve's situation was different. They were innocent but had not been made righteous *by Christ*. We, on the other hand, become righteous through Christ's atonement.

1. If Adam and Eve sinned while living in Eden, how do we know that we won't sin in Heaven and bring about another Fall? What will make our situation in Heaven different from Adam and Eve's in Eden?

_____

_____

_____

2. How will seeing God, his creation, and ourselves for what they—and we—really are affect how we think and choose?

_____

_____

_____

_____

3. Based on Revelation 21:8, 27 and 22:15, what bearing will evil have on people in Heaven? (See *Heaven,* p. 300, or p. 312 in revised edition.)

_____

_____

_____

_____

_____

4. Review the discussion of perfection on pp. 302–303 of *Heaven* (pp. 314–315 in revised edition). In what sense will we be perfect in Heaven, and in what sense will we not?

_____

_____

_____

_____

5. "Our greatest deliverance in Heaven will be from *ourselves.*" In what sense is this true? (See *Heaven,* p. 303, or p. 315 in revised edition.)

_____

_____

_____

_____

CHAPTER 32
What Will We Know and Learn?

God alone is omniscient. When we die, we'll see things far more clearly, and we'll know much more than we do now, but we'll never know everything. . . . God alone sees clearly and comprehensively. In Heaven we'll see far more clearly, but we'll never see comprehensively. The point of comparing our knowing to God's knowing is that we'll know "fully" in the sense of accurately but not exhaustively.

1. Will we ever know as much as God does? Explain the difference between seeing *clearly* and seeing *comprehensively.*

_____

_____

_____

2. Do you agree or disagree that Ephesians 2:6-7 indicates we will always be learning in eternity?

_____

_____

_____

3. How do you feel about the idea of always learning more, rather than instantly knowing all we will ever know?

_____

_____

_____

_____

4. "There's so much to discover in this universe, but we have so little time and opportunity" (*Heaven,* p. 310, or p. 322 in revised edition). When the limitations of our temporal lives are removed in Heaven, what kinds of things might you want to learn?

_____

_____

_____

5. Based on what you read in the book of Revelation, what do you know about the books that will be in Heaven? What do you believe about whether we might read and write books on the New Earth? (See *Heaven,* pp. 311–315, or pp. 323–327 in revised edition.) Explain your answer.

_____

_____

_____

6. Will we all have the same knowledge and skill levels in Heaven in every area? Why or why not? How does the doctrine of continuity and God's gifting and personal preference play into this?

_____

_____

_____

CHAPTER 33
What Will Our Daily Lives Be Like?

Eden is a picture of rest—work that's meaningful and enjoyable, abundant food, a beautiful environment, unhindered friendship with God and other people and animals. Even with Eden's restful perfection, one day was set aside for special rest and worship. Work will be refreshing on the New Earth, yet regular rest will be built into our lives.

1. Why is it important to have a day of rest in our weekly schedules, and how does that relate to the restfulness of Heaven? (See Matthew 11:28 and Hebrews 4:11.)

_____

_____

_____

2. How would you respond to someone who says, "Heaven is about rest, and resting all the time means inactivity and boredom"?

_____

_____

_____

3. According to Genesis 2:15, was work a part of the Curse? How was work affected by the Curse? (See Genesis 3:17-19.)

_____

_____

_____

4. God says of the New Earth, "No longer will there be any curse. The throne of God and of the Lamb will be in the city, and his servants will serve him . . . and they will reign for ever and ever" (Revelation 22:3, 5). *Serve* and *reign* are verbs denoting distinct kinds of action. What do you conclude from the fact that we will serve and reign on the New Earth for ever and ever?

_____

_____

_____

5. Prior to this study, as you thought about Heaven, did you envision activity and work there? How does this idea make you feel?

_____

_____

_____

_____

6. What does Luke 16:9, in context, seem to indicate about the presence of homes and the practice of hospitality on the New Earth? What do you imagine these will be like?

_____

_____

_____

_____

SECTION TEN: WHAT WILL OUR RELATIONSHIPS BE LIKE?

CHAPTER 34
Will We Desire Relationships with Anyone Except God?

Some people falsely assume that when we give attention to people, it automatically distracts us from God. But even now, in a fallen world, people can turn my attention toward God. Was Jesus distracted from God by spending time with people on Earth? Certainly not. In Heaven, no person will distract us from God. We will never experience any conflict between worshiping God himself and enjoying God's people.

1. If God is sufficient to meet all our needs, why will we still have relationships with people in Heaven? (See Genesis 2:18.)

_____

_____

_____

2. On this earth, we are tempted to make idols out of people and things, putting them before God. Will we have those temptations in Heaven? Once we're in God's presence, how will people and things created by God affect our relationship with him?

_____

_____

_____

3. Among people you've known on Earth, who are you most looking forward to seeing in Heaven? Where might you want to go with them, and what might you want to do with them on the New Earth?

_____

_____

_____

4. In Heaven, will we remember our lives on the old Earth? If so, then how do we explain what it says in Isaiah 65:17 about former things not being remembered? (See *Heaven,* pp. 330–331, or pp. 343–345 in revised edition.)

_____

_____

_____

5. How do christoplatonic assumptions affect our views about relationships in Heaven? (See *Heaven,* p. 332, or p. 345 in revised edition, and Appendix A.)

_____

_____

_____

6. People often wonder whether we will recognize one another in Heaven. What are the arguments pro and con? Do you agree or disagree that if we won't know our loved ones in Heaven, the "comfort" of an afterlife reunion taught in 1 Thessalonians 4:14-18 would be of no comfort at all? (See *Heaven*, p. 333, or pp. 345–347 in revised edition.)

_____

_____

_____

_____

CHAPTER 35
Will There Be Marriage, Families, and Friendships?

Receiving glorified bodies and relocating to the New Earth won't erase history, it will culminate history. Nothing will negate or minimize the fact that we were members of families on the old Earth. . . . Resurrection bodies will presumably have chromosomes and DNA, with a signature that forever testifies to our genetic connection with family.

1. Read Mark 10:29-30. What does it mean to you that we'll all be part of one big family in Heaven?

_____

_____

_____

_____

_____

2. In Matthew 22:29-30, what does Jesus teach about marriage in Heaven? Do you agree that instead of there being *no* marriage in Heaven, there will be *one* marriage?

_____

_____

_____

_____

3. Do you believe that being married to Christ will draw *all* your relationships closer? (See *Heaven*, p. 336, or pp. 350–351 in revised edition.) Is it possible that, next to Jesus himself, someone's best friend on the New Earth will be the person to whom he or she was married on the old Earth? Is it possible that parents and children will enjoy very close relationships in Heaven, closer even than the ones they have now?

_____

_____

_____

4. What is your understanding of the reasons why we'll have distinct genders in Heaven but will not engage in sexual relationships? Do you agree or disagree that God would not eliminate sex without replacing it with something better?

_____

_____

_____

5. Review the section titled "Will We Be Reunited with Infants Who Have Died?" (See *Heaven*, pp. 340–342, or pp. 354–356 in revised edition.) Record any concepts presented here that are new to you or that you wish to discuss.

_____

_____

_____

CHAPTER 36

Whom Will We Meet, and What Will We Experience Together?

Wouldn't it be great to travel to Heaven together, simultaneously? Wouldn't it be great to be like Lewis and Clark, discovering *together* the wonders of the new world? In fact, that's precisely what Scripture tells us will happen. Though we go to the present Heaven one at a time as we die, *all of us* will be charter citizens of the New Earth. We'll be resurrected together and set foot on the New Earth together.

1. What activities might you enjoy doing with both new and old friends and family?

_____

_____

_____

2. To whom do you want to say "Thank you" in Heaven?

_____

_____

_____

3. If some people we loved on Earth are in Hell, will that spoil our experience of Heaven? Why or why not? (See 2 Corinthians 1:3 and Revelation 21:4.)

_____

_____

_____

_____

4. What does Revelation 18:20 suggest about how people in Heaven feel about God executing judgment on sinners?

_____

_____

_____

_____

5. "Because we're finite and unique and because we'll never know everything, we may not agree about everything in Heaven" (*Heaven*, p. 348, or p. 363 in revised edition). In the absence of sin and selfishness, do you think there could still be disagreements or differences of opinion between people whose knowledge is finite? How would disagreements be resolved?

_____

_____

_____

_____

CHAPTER 37
How Will We Relate to Each Other?

Any vision of the afterlife that doesn't involve a society of human beings in meaningful relationship denies God's decree that it isn't good for human beings to be without others of their kind. It also denies innumerable Scripture passages that clearly reveal human society on the New Earth.

1. Jonathan Edwards, the great Puritan preacher, said, "The saints are like so many vessels of different sizes cast into a sea of happiness where every vessel is full: this is eternal life, for a man ever to

have his capacity filled. But after all 'tis left to God's sovereign pleasure, 'tis his prerogative to determine the largeness of the vessel." What does this quote suggest about how we will all be equal in Heaven without all being the same? Is there anything we can do to affect the size of our heavenly "vessel"? (See Matthew 6:19-20; 25:14-29; and 1 Corinthians 3:12-15.)

_____

_____

_____

_____

2. Do you believe there will be privacy in Heaven? Why or why not?

_____

_____

_____

_____

3. What does the Bible say that suggests there will be private ownership in Heaven? (See Daniel 12:13; Matthew 6:20; Luke 16:9; Colossians 3:24; Revelation 2:17; and 21:7.)

_____

_____

_____

_____

4. What do you think of the possibility that in Heaven we will regain lost relational opportunities?

_____

_____

_____

_____

5. If you are a Christian, describe what you think your first day will be like in the intermediate, or present, Heaven (where Christians go when they die).

_____

_____

_____

_____

6. Describe what you think your first day on the New Earth will be like. What might you see? What broken things will be fixed, or sicknesses healed? Where might you want to go, and what will you want to do? What will your relationship with Christ be like? Will you look forward to the future?

_____

_____

_____

_____

CHAPTER 38

What Will New Earth Society Be Like?

The New Earth will include not only resurrected geographical locations but also resurrected cultures. The kings of the nations will bring their tribute, splendor, and glory into the New Jerusalem. There will be not one nation but many. . . . The best culture, history, art, and music of the old Earth will be redeemed, purified, and carried over to the New Earth.

1. What kind of diversity in Heaven is indicated by Revelation 7:9-10?

_____

_____

_____

_____

2. What can we do now to get a head start on the kind of unity between races that we will experience in Heaven?

_____

_____

_____

_____

3. Discuss the role of languages in Heaven. Do you think diverse languages will be abolished, or might they continue? Does it make sense that we will have one central common language in Heaven even if we know other languages? Why?

_____

_____

_____

_____

4. Read Revelation 21:24-26. What do these verses teach about the presence of distinct nations, with their own rulers, on the New Earth?

_____

_____

_____

_____

5. If modern nations will exist on the New Earth, what about ancient nations that no longer exist on Earth? Does it make sense

to you that ancient and bygone cultures will be represented in Heaven? Why or why not? (Which past cultures would you be most interested in visiting and learning about on the New Earth?)

_____

_____

_____

_____

CHAPTER 39
Will Animals Inhabit the New Earth?

God's plan for a renewed Earth after the Flood emphatically involved animals. Wouldn't we expect his plan for a renewed Earth after the future judgment to likewise include animals? If the rescue of mankind in the ark is a picture of redemption, doesn't the rescue of the animals in the ark also anticipate their restoration as part of God's redemptive purposes?

1. What do animals and people have in common? How are they different?

_____

_____

_____

_____

2. Read Genesis 1:30; 2:7; 6:17-20; and 7:15, 21-22. What do these passages suggest about the special nature of animals?

_____

_____

_____

_____

3. Read Genesis 9:9-17. What does this passage say about God's view of animals and their connection with humans? How does this perspective affect how we think about and treat animals? (Clearly, some people overestimate the value of animals, putting them on the same level as people. But do some other people *underestimate* the value of animals to God?)

_____

_____

_____

_____

4. Read Psalms 148:10-13 and 150:6. What important directive have animals been given? (See *Heaven,* pp. 378–380, or pp. 392–394 in revised edition.)

_____

_____

_____

_____

5. Some people interpret Isaiah 11:6-9 and 65:25 as relating only to the millennial kingdom. Do you think these passages speak only of the Millennium, the New Earth, or both? Why?

_____

_____

_____

_____

6. Explain the importance of animals on the present Earth and how their care and management is a major part of the responsibilities that God entrusted to mankind. How would you expect this to be similar or different on the New Earth?

_____

_____

_____

_____

CHAPTER 40
Will Animals, Including Our Pets, Live Again?

Did Christ die for animals? Certainly not in the way he died for mankind. People are made in God's image, animals aren't. People sinned, animals didn't. Because animals didn't sin, they don't need a redeemer in the same way. But in another sense, Christ died for animals indirectly because his death for humanity purchased redemption for what was brought down by humanity's sin, including animals.

1. Is it right or wrong to grieve the death of our pets? Is the attachment that people feel to their animals primarily a result of Creation or the Fall? Explain.

_____

_____

_____

_____

2. Did Adam and Eve have a higher or a lower regard for animals than most people have had since Eden? Why is this significant?

_____

_____

_____

_____

3. What did John Wesley say in the sermon he preached in 1781 about animals? (See *Heaven,* pp. 388–389, or pp. 402–403 in revised edition.) What is your response to his thoughts?

_____

_____

_____

_____

4. From the statement in Genesis 3:1 about the talking serpent being "more crafty" than other animals in Eden, what can we surmise about the original level of animal intelligence?

_____

_____

_____

_____

5. Does Romans 8:18-23 suggest the possibility that some animals now alive (perhaps including pets) might live again on the New Earth, raised "on the coattails" of our resurrection? What in the text either supports or refutes this idea?

_____

_____

_____

_____

CHAPTER 41
Will Heaven Ever Be Boring?

God calls us to follow him in an adventure that should put us on life's edge. He's infinite in creativity, goodness, beauty, and power. If we're experiencing the invigorating stirrings of God's Spirit, trusting him to fill our lives with divine appointments, experiencing the childlike delights of his gracious daily kindnesses, then we'll know that God is exciting and Heaven is exhilarating. People who love God crave his companionship. To be in his presence will be the very opposite of boredom.

1. Read Psalm 16:11. What does it say about what we will experience in God's presence?

_____

_____

_____

_____

2. What indications does the Bible give us that Heaven will not be boring? In your heart, do you believe it's true? Where do we get the idea that Heaven might be boring? Does it suggest we believe that God is boring?

_____

_____

_____

_____

3. Why do some Christians struggle with the idea of having fun in Heaven? What does this say about how our churches and Christian families portray Heaven?

_____

_____

_____

_____

4. What do you think of the idea that your life's work will continue in Heaven? If you are presently employed in a job that depends on aspects of our fallen world (and thus will not exist on the New Earth), or if your job is not consistent with your true passion or calling, what kind of work do you think or hope you might do on the New Earth?

_____

_____

_____

_____

5. Explain the difference between "lifeboat" theology and "ark" theology concerning this life and the next. Is your theology of life on Earth a lifeboat theology or an ark theology? Which do you think is more biblical?

_____

_____

_____

_____

_____

CHAPTER 42
Will There Be Arts, Entertainment, and Sports?

Music, dancing, storytelling, art, entertainment, drama, and books have played major roles in human culture. Will they remain a part of our lives on the New Earth? I'm convinced the answer is yes. . . . In Heaven, God will unleash our creativity, not confine it.

1. Why is it reasonable to expect cultural elements such as music, dance, stories, and the arts to continue when we are resurrected beings living on the New Earth?

_____

_____

_____

_____

2. What biblical passage clearly demonstrates that there will be laughter in Heaven?

_____

_____

_____

_____

3. What kind of laughter will there likely be in Heaven? What kind will not be there? Give examples of God-honoring kinds of laughter.

_____

_____

_____

4. Do storytelling, creativity, and sports result from our sinfulness or our humanity? When we live on the New Earth as resurrected beings, will we *still* be human? If so, what does this suggest about the kinds of things we will do and want to do?

_____

_____

_____

_____

5. Is there anything inherently bad about sports? What bearing do 1 Corinthians 9:24-27 and 2 Timothy 2:5 have on this question? Does playing a game or engaging in competition demand having a sin nature or a bad attitude? Why or why not? Would people on the New Earth be tempted to get angry and jealous and insecure if they played sports? If Adam and Eve hadn't sinned, would an unfallen culture have invented and played sports?

_____

_____

_____

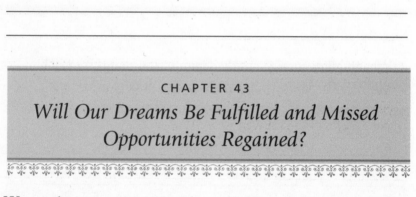

CHAPTER 43
Will Our Dreams Be Fulfilled and Missed Opportunities Regained?

We use the term *eternal life* without thinking what it means. Life is an earthly existence in which we work, rest, play, and relate to each other in ways that include the cultivation and enjoyment of culture. Yet we have redefined eternal life to mean an off-Earth existence stripped of the defining properties of what we know life to be. Eternal life will be enjoying forever what life on Earth . . . at its finest moments . . . was intended to be.

1. Do you have unfulfilled dreams that you would love to see fulfilled on the New Earth? Do you think some of them will be? Why or why not?

_____

_____

_____

2. How will the measurement of success be different in Heaven than it is on Earth?

_____

_____

_____

3. What do you think about the statement, "The better we use our time and opportunity for God's glory now, the greater will be our opportunities there" (*Heaven*, p. 420, or p. 436 in revised edition)? Consider Luke 16:11-12 and 19:17 in formulating your answer.

_____

_____

_____

4. What are we commanded to do in Matthew 6:19-21? What does this suggest about the relationship between the choices we make today and the Heaven we will experience forever?

_____

_____

_____

5. How does the example of the dot and the line (see *Heaven*, p. 420, or p. 436 in revised edition) affect your perspective on this life and the next? How does it affect how you live here and now? How should it?

_____

_____

_____

CHAPTER 44

Will We Design Crafts, Technology, and New Modes of Travel?

God is a maker. He'll never cease being a maker. God made us, his image-bearers, to be makers. We'll never cease to be makers. When we die, we won't leave behind our creativity, but only what hinders our ability to honor God through what we create.

1. When you consider that the New Earth may include much that is part of our lives today—including technology, travel, and perhaps even a modified form of business—are you encouraged or disappointed? Do you feel that you've had enough of these things on the present Earth? Explain how you think these and other things will be different on the New Earth.

_____

_____

_____

_____

_____

2. If you were going to describe the eternal Heaven to someone who had never heard of it, what would you say? Is your explanation any different after reading this book than it was before you read it? Explain.

_____

_____

_____

_____

_____

3. What truth in Colossians 3:23-24 motivates you in your present work and as you anticipate your future work on the New Earth?

_____

_____

_____

_____

_____

4. All technology, machinery, and vehicles on the present Earth are products of the dreams, designs, and creativity of fallen humans who are nonetheless made in God's image. On the New Earth, when we're free of corruption, sin, and the Curse, what kinds of things do you think we'll design and do? What ideas do you have that you might want to pursue? Where would you like to go if outer space travel or time travel were possible?

_____

_____

_____

_____

_____

PART III
LIVING IN LIGHT
OF HEAVEN

CHAPTER 45
Reorienting Ourselves to Heaven as Our Home

We need to stop acting as if Heaven were a myth, an impossible dream, a relentlessly dull meeting, or an unimportant distraction from real life. We need to see Heaven for what it is: the realm we were made for. If we do, we'll embrace the prospect of Heaven with contagious joy, excitement, and anticipation.

1. Heaven will include good things about our earthly homes, without any of the bad. What elements of "home" do you expect to see in Heaven?

_____

_____

_____

_____

2. What factors inhibit our ability to see Heaven as "home"? Do you think our failure to understand the doctrine of the New Earth is a large part of it?

_____

_____

_____

_____

3. Has this chapter helped you think differently about terminal illness and "premature" death, especially in terms of the "party" going on in Heaven?

_____

_____

_____

_____

4. Read Luke 6:22-23; Colossians 1:24; James 1:2; and 1 Peter 4:13. How do these verses address the misconceptions of the "health and wealth" gospel? (See *Heaven,* p. 444, or p. 460 in revised edition.)

_____

_____

_____

_____

5. Explain how we can have a longing—and even a sort of nostalgia—for life on the New Earth, even though we haven't yet experienced it.

_____

_____

_____

_____

6. "We see life differently when we realize that death isn't a wall but a turnstile, a small obstacle that marks a great beginning" (*Heaven*, p. 447, or p. 463 in revised edition). How has your study of *Heaven* affected your perspective about life on this earth, death, and eternal life on the New Earth?

_____

_____

_____

_____

CHAPTER 46
Anticipating the Great Adventure

The most ordinary moment on the New Earth will be greater than the most perfect moments in this life—those experiences you wanted to bottle or hang on to but couldn't. It *can* get better, far better, than this—*and it will*. Life on the New Earth will be like sitting in front of the fire with family and friends, basking in the warmth, laughing uproariously, dreaming of the adventures to come—and then going out and *living* those adventures together. With no fear that life will ever end or that tragedy will descend like a dark cloud. With no fear that dreams will be shattered or relationships broken.

1. What purposes does God have for keeping us here on Earth for the time being?

_____

_____

_____

_____

2. If Heaven is so wonderful and life is too painful, what's wrong with taking one's own life to get to Heaven more quickly?

_____

_____

_____

3. What are some ways in which we can prepare *now* for eternal life in Heaven? (See Galatians 6:7-10; Philippians 3:13-14; Hebrews 12:28; 2 Peter 3:11-14; and 1 John 3:3.)

_____

_____

_____

4. Jot down some of the truths about the New Earth found in Revelation 21–22. What especially stands out to you?

_____

_____

_____

5. Looking back at your study of *Heaven*, what are some of the key things that you have learned from Scripture and from the book?

_____

_____

_____

6. How has this study motivated you to live differently? Consider 2 Peter 3:11-14.

_____

_____

_____

Christoplatonism's False Assumptions

Because of Christoplatonism's pervasive influence, we resist the biblical picture of bodily resurrection of the dead and life on the New Earth; of eating and drinking in Heaven; of walking and talking, living in dwelling places, traveling down streets, and going through gates from one place to another; and of ruling, working, playing, and engaging in earthly culture.

1. The term *Christoplatonism* refers to the adoption of Platonic Greek philosophy by some of the early church fathers, causing them to see biblical teachings about resurrection and the New Earth as allegorical and non-material. Has Christoplatonism, whether or not you have consciously embraced it, had an influence on your view of resurrection, the New Earth, and what we will do in eternity? If so, in what ways?

_____

_____

_____

_____

_____

2. For Plato, the human body was a hindrance to or a prison for the spirit. It was considered to be in opposition to the soul. "But according to Scripture, our bodies aren't just shells for our spirits to inhabit; they're a good and essential aspect of our being. Likewise, the earth is not a second-rate location from which we must be delivered. Rather, it was handmade by God for us. Earth, not some incorporeal state, is God's choice as mankind's original and ultimate dwelling place" (*Heaven*, p. 459, or p. 475 in revised edition). Do you agree or disagree with this statement? How can our

perspective on this subject affect our view of what Heaven will be like and what we'll be like in Heaven?

_____

_____

_____

_____

_____

3. "The Incarnation wasn't God talking *as if* he'd become a man—it was God actually becoming a man. The doctrine of the bodily resurrection of the dead isn't God telling us we'll have bodies because that's all we're capable of understanding. We really *will* have bodies. The doctrine of the New Earth isn't God acting as if we'll live in an earthly realm—rather, it's God explicitly telling us that we *will* live on the New Earth. . . . The New Earth will be a real Earth where mankind and God will dwell together" (*Heaven*, pp. 462–463, or pp. 478–479 in revised edition). Do you agree or disagree? How does this affect your understanding of eternal life?

_____

_____

_____

_____

4. What are some concepts taught in the Bible that refute the philosophy of Christoplatonism?

_____

_____

_____

_____

Literal and Figurative Interpretation

No one interprets the Bible absolutely literally or absolutely figuratively. Whether we tend more toward the literal or the figurative depends largely on our assumptions. . . . Obviously, there are many figures of speech in the Bible, such as when Peter is called a rock and Christ is called a door, a lamb with seven eyes, or has a sword coming out of his mouth. Scripture is also full of accounts that should be taken literally. . . . Paying attention to context and taking other Scriptures into account, we need to draw God's truth from the text, not superimpose our preconceived ideas onto it.

1. Summarize and comment on the following statement: "We read in Luke 15:7 that Jesus says there is 'rejoicing in heaven over one sinner who repents,' yet we don't believe that people in Heaven are aware of what's happening to people on Earth. We read in Luke 16:9 that we should 'use worldly wealth to gain friends for yourselves, so that when it is gone, you will be welcomed into eternal dwellings,' yet we don't believe we'll have homes in Heaven and open those homes to each other. We read passages in the prophets promising that God's people will live forever on a righteous Earth, then assume this must mean a spiritual blessing in an incorporeal Heaven. We read that we will have resurrection bodies and will eat and drink at tables with Christ and fellow believers, yet we don't actually envision this to be true. We read in the last two chapters of Revelation about nations on the New Earth and kings of those nations bringing their treasures into the city, yet we don't believe there will be real nations or kings of those nations. Many doubt there will be a city at all. The examples go on and on—when it comes to the eternal state, we don't let Scripture say what it says" (*Heaven*, pp. 467–468, or pp. 483–484 in revised edition).

_____

_____

_____

_____

2. Many passages of Scripture are figurative (e.g., Jesus being called the Lamb of God, the Door, the Good Shepherd, and the Bread of Life), and it is typically obvious that they are figurative. Do you think that passages that talk about the New Earth; the resurrection body; and eating, drinking, serving, and reigning together in God's Kingdom on Earth should be taken figuratively or literally? How can you tell when to use one approach or the other?

_____

_____

_____

_____

3. "The scholastic view gradually replaced the old, more literal understanding of Heaven as garden and city, a place of earthly beauty, dwelling places, food, and fellowship. The loss was incalculable. The church to this day has never recovered from the unearthly—and anti-earthly—theology of Heaven constructed by well-meaning but misguided scholastic theologians. These men interpreted biblical revelation not in a straightforward manner, but in light of the intellectually seductive notions of Platonism, Stoicism, and Gnosticism" (_Heaven,_ p. 469, or p. 485 in revised edition). Does this help explain how Christians can read the Bible and hear it taught for years, yet never develop a grasp of what it actually teaches about the resurrection and the New Earth?

_____

_____

_____

_____

4. What have you learned from the discussion about literal and figurative interpretation? How does it help you interpret what the Bible says about Heaven?

_____

_____

_____

_____

NOTES

NOTES

NOTES

ABOUT THE AUTHOR

Dr. Randy Alcorn is the founder and director of Eternal Perspective Ministries (EPM), a nonprofit ministry devoted to promoting an eternal viewpoint and drawing attention to people in special need of advocacy and help.

A pastor for fourteen years before founding EPM in 1990, Randy is a popular teacher and conference speaker. He has spoken in a number of countries and has been interviewed on more than 600 radio and television programs. Holding degrees in theology and biblical studies, he has taught biblical interpretation, theology, and ethics on the adjunct faculties of Multnomah University and Western Seminary in Portland, Oregon.

Randy is the author of more than thirty books (4 million in print), including *Heaven; The Treasure Principle; The Grace and Truth Paradox; The Purity Principle; In Light of Eternity: Perspectives on Heaven; ProLife Answers to ProChoice Arguments; Money, Possessions, and Eternity; The Law of Rewards;* and *Why ProLife?* His novels include *Deadline, Dominion, Deception, Edge of Eternity, Lord Foulgrin's Letters, The Ishbane Conspiracy* (coauthored with his daughters), and the 2002 Gold Medallion winner for best novel of the year, *Safely Home.*

Randy lives in Gresham, Oregon, with his wife, Nanci. They have two grown daughters, Karina Franklin and Angela Stump, and several grandchildren.

Eternal Perspective Ministries contact information:
Web site: www.epm.org
E-mail: info@epm.org
Phone: 503-668-5200
Mail: 39085 Pioneer Blvd., Suite 200, Sandy, OR 97055

Follow Randy Alcorn online:
www.randyalcorn.blogspot.com
www.facebook.com/randyalcorn
www.twitter.com/randyalcorn

OTHER BOOKS BY RANDY ALCORN

FICTION

Deadline

Dominion

Deception

Edge of Eternity

Lord Foulgrin's Letters

The Ishbane Conspiracy

Safely Home

NONFICTION

Touchpoints: Heaven

50 Days of Heaven

In Light of Eternity

Money, Possessions, and Eternity

The Law of Rewards

ProLife Answers to ProChoice Arguments

Sexual Temptation

The Grace and Truth Paradox

The Purity Principle

The Treasure Principle

Why ProLife?

If God Is Good

KIDS

Heaven for Kids

Wait Until Then

Tell Me About Heaven

Take the Heaven IQ Quiz
at www.heaveniq.com/books

CP0143

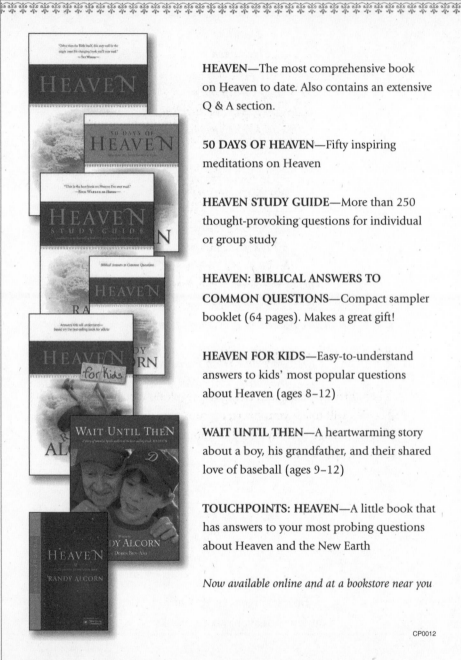

HEAVEN—The most comprehensive book on Heaven to date. Also contains an extensive Q & A section.

50 DAYS OF HEAVEN—Fifty inspiring meditations on Heaven

HEAVEN STUDY GUIDE—More than 250 thought-provoking questions for individual or group study

HEAVEN: BIBLICAL ANSWERS TO COMMON QUESTIONS—Compact sampler booklet (64 pages). Makes a great gift!

HEAVEN FOR KIDS—Easy-to-understand answers to kids' most popular questions about Heaven (ages 8–12)

WAIT UNTIL THEN—A heartwarming story about a boy, his grandfather, and their shared love of baseball (ages 9–12)

TOUCHPOINTS: HEAVEN—A little book that has answers to your most probing questions about Heaven and the New Earth

Now available online and at a bookstore near you

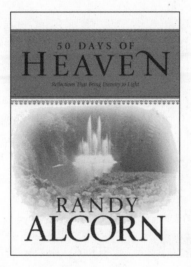

50 DAYS OF HEAVEN

These fifty inspiring and thought-provoking meditations on Heaven will touch your heart, capture your imagination, and forever change the way you think about the spectacular new universe that awaits us!

CP0013

LOOK FOR THESE TYNDALE BOOKS
BY RANDY ALCORN
AT YOUR LOCAL BOOKSTORE

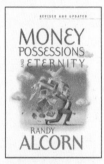

MONEY, POSSESSIONS, AND ETERNITY

This classic best seller provides a thoroughly biblical perspective about money and material possessions. Includes a study guide and appendix with additional resources.

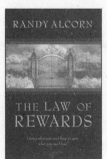

THE LAW OF REWARDS

Using excerpts from his classic *Money, Possessions, and Eternity*, Randy Alcorn demonstrates that believers will receive differing rewards in Heaven depending on their actions and choices here on Earth.

SAFELY HOME

"Not only is *Safely Home* a first-class story, it's also a bracing wake-up call about Christian persecution in China. You'll be challenged."
—CHARLES COLSON

"This brilliant story mixes the warmth of a good novel with the harsh reality of the persecuted church."
—DR. TIM LAHAYE

CP0124